The Blossom on the Bough

A BOOK OF TREES

FLOWERING DOGWOOD

ANNE OPHELIA DOWDEN

The Blossom on the Bough

A BOOK OF TREES

TICKNOR & FIELDS *Books for Young Readers* New York 1994

AMERICAN
HORNBEAM

Published by Ticknor & Fields Books for Young Readers, A Houghton Mifflin company, 215 Park Avenue South, New York, New York 10003.

All plants pictured in this book—except enlarged details—are exactly 3/5 natural size.

The map on page 64 is by Miklos Pinther.
A portion of this book, including a number of the color illustrations, first appeared in *Audubon* magazine.

Manufactured in the United States of America
The text of this book is set in 14 point Egmont Light
The illustrations are watercolor, reproduced in full color and black and white

HOR   10   9   8   7   6   5   4   3   2   1

Library of Congress Cataloging-in-Publication Data

Dowden, Anne Ophelia Todd.
The blossom on the bough : a book of trees / by Anne Ophelia Dowden.
p. cm. Reprint. Originally published: New York : Crowell, c1975. Includes index. Summary: Discusses the importance of forests, the parts and cycles of trees, the functions of flowers and fruits, the distinctive features of conifers, and the forest regions in the United States.
ISBN 0-395-68375-0 (cl) — ISBN 0-395-68943-0 (pa)
1. Trees—Juvenile literature. 2. Trees—United States—Juvenile literature. 3. Forests and forestry—United States—Juvenile literature. [1. Trees. 2. Forests and forestry.] I. Title.   [QK475.8.D68 1994]   582.16097—dc20
93-22726   CIP   AC

ACKNOWLEDGMENTS

Any study of trees, but especially a close-up study of their flowers and fruits, involves mechanical problems not encountered in other botanical pursuits. The more stately and important the tree, the higher it holds its flowering branches; and specimens for painting are hard to come by if one is not agile at climbing. Collecting all the flowers and fruits illustrated in this book would never have been possible without the help of a great many people: at the Brooklyn Botanic Garden, Mr. Edmond Moulin, Mr. Tom Dellendick, Dr. Stephen K-M Tim; at the New York Botanical Garden, Mr. Harry Goode, Mr. Joseph Kilz; at Callaway Gardens, Pine Mountain, Georgia, Mr. Fred Galle, Dr. Frank Willingham; at the University of California, Riverside, the Drs. John and Betty Moore; in Boulder, Colorado, Miss Helen Harper; in Springfield, Vermont, Mr. and Mrs. Stuart Eldredge.

I am also greatly indebted to Dr. Louis C. Wheeler, Department of Biological Science, University of Southern California, Los Angeles, and Mr. Frederick McGourty, editor of *Plants and Gardens*, Brooklyn Botanic Garden, who gave advice botanical and editorial; to Dr. Peter K. Nelson, Department of Biology, Brooklyn College, who read my manuscript and gave invaluable aid with many problems of plant physiology; to Mr. Frederick Page, Professor of Botany Emeritus, Dartmouth College, who helped in the search for specimens and then in their identification; to Mr. George Kalmbacher, Taxonomist, Brooklyn Botanic Garden, who not only helped with identification of specimens but also monitored the blooming of dozens of trees at the Garden and signaled their availability for painting; to Miss Edith B. Todd and Miss Myra Kelley, who assisted on collecting trips to the country; and to my husband, Raymond B. Dowden, whose enthusiasm for this work went far beyond the woods and fields we roamed together, who sometimes in exasperation titled the book "Go Climb a Tree," but who did in fact help solve the gymnastics attendant upon a project so far over our heads.

BLACKHAW

Merrily, merrily shall I live now
Under the blossom that hangs on the bough.
                    —The Tempest

CONTENTS

WHITE ASH

Staminate flowers

Pistillate flowers

Fruits (samaras)

OUR FOREST HERITAGE

The oldest living things on earth are trees. Some of California's sequoias have for four thousand years looked down on the changes in the landscape and the comings and goings of mankind. They sprouted from tiny seeds about the time the Egyptian pyramids were being built. They were sturdy young saplings when Moses led the Israelites to the Promised Land. Today these giant patriarchs seem as remote and inaccessible as the rocks and mountain cliffs on which they grow, like cathedral columns holding up the sky. It is hard to imagine them playing any part in the lives of mere humans or being in any way affected by the creatures that pass at their feet.

Lesser trees, however, have played an intimate role in the life of man since he first appeared on earth. In his remote beginnings, trees were perhaps the most important part of his environment. They fed the fires that warmed him; they gave him shelter, food, and medicine, and even clothing. They also shaped his spiritual horizons. Trees expressed for him the grandeur and mystery of life, as they moved through the cycle of seasons, from life to death and back to life again. They were the largest living things around him. He knew that some of

1

them had been standing on the same spot in his father's time and in his grandfather's, and would continue to stand long after he was gone. No wonder these trees became symbols of strength, fruitfulness, and everlasting life.

The idea of a Tree of Life began with the beginning of civilization, in Asia Minor, and through the centuries the concept was taken up by religions throughout the world. Sometimes the Tree of Life was purely imaginary, like no living plant; sometimes it was a real tree—the oak, the ash, and the fir in Northern Europe or the palm and the cedar in the Middle East. Many trees were considered sacred for other reasons: they were believed to house wood gods or spirits, or they were connected with the lives of prophets or saints. In their symbolic roles, trees continue to have a place in nearly all present-day religions.

Association with trees is still an uplifting and purifying experience, but it is becoming less and less a part of American life. We now tend to value trees because of their practical usefulness. They provide us with a strong, durable, and easily worked building material; with wood for beautiful furniture; with pulp for the paper of millions of newspapers, magazines, and cartons; with lumber for posts and pilings. In some parts of the world, though not in the United States, they also provide most of the fuel.

The demand for wood in America has from the beginning been enormous. The earliest settlers found vast forests that covered almost half the land area of the country. It seemed like an inexhaustible supply of timber, and they cut it freely, first to clear land for farms and homes, and then to get lumber. As cities and highways spread and industrial needs grew, immense areas were shorn of their trees and left bare and eroding. No one thought about the future or worried about the valuable

2

resource they were destroying. But, though nature does restore herself and trees always return, it takes at least a hundred years to grow a new forest. And even then, the new community of plants will not be the same as it was in the virgin forest. Only a few thousand acres of these virgin forests remain, mostly in the West.

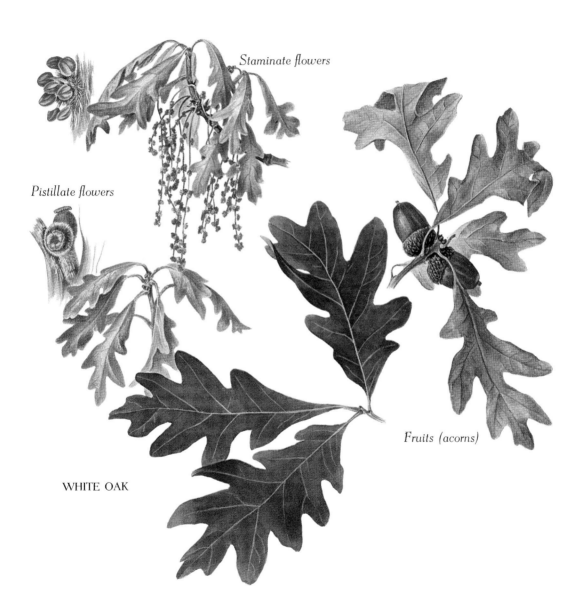

Staminate flowers

Pistillate flowers

Fruits (acorns)

WHITE OAK

Finally, in the early 1900's, people became alarmed by the rapid destruction of their woodlands. They took a lesson in forestry from Europe and began to grow and harvest trees as they did other crops. Today about a third of the United States is covered with second-growth forests—some natural, some planted. The planted ones are always composed of a single kind of tree, which results in a monotony very different from the glorious variety of the original woods.

But these second-growth forests are better than nothing, because a world without trees might be a world without life. Trees provide far more important things than lumber and paper. They affect the climate in which we live, changing temperatures and releasing quantities of water into the air. They control the flow of water over the ground and hold the soil in place against erosion. They change the character of the land as their roots slowly break up rocks to form new soil. Each year they deposit tons of organic matter in the form of leaves that will rot away and return a great store of minerals to the earth from which they originally came. Trees shelter and nourish whole communities of plants and animals. But, most important of all, the green world of plants provides animals and human beings with all the oxygen they breathe. This vital gas is released into the air as a by-product of the life process of all plants. A patch of grass, a field of clover, a growing tree—all give us, literally, the breath of life.

The chemical activity going on inside a great tree is truly stupendous. By virtue of this activity, a massive amount of living material unfolds in midair, nourishing itself with gases and minerals, giving life to other creatures. With all our scientific knowledge, we must marvel at the growth of a tree ; no wonder our ancestors found it worthy of reverence and even of worship.

BLACK CHERRY

A TREE IS A PLANT

Most people know a tree only as a large mass of green leaves supported by the heavy column of its trunk. Many are not aware that trees like sycamore, oak, and elm are flowering plants as truly as a buttercup is. The sycamore has the same parts as a buttercup—roots, stem, leaves, and flowers—and these parts serve the same purposes. The differences between the two plants (and there are, of course, some enormous differences) are nearly all related to the great size and long life of the tree.

5

SYCAMORE

Pistillate flowers

Staminate flowers

"Seeds" (achenes)

"Seeds" (achenes)

A buttercup plant and a sycamore tree both grow from seeds of about the same size. As each seed starts to grow, it pushes down a tiny root, sends up a tiny shoot, spreads two tiny seed-leaves, and then continues to grow upward, with a steady spreading of new leaves. Eventually it is old enough to flower, to form new seeds, and to start the cycle over again. In a butter-cup, this is accomplished in one season. With the arrival of cold weather, the plant dies down. In some buttercups, the root lives on, to send up a new flowering stalk in the spring; in others, the whole plant dies, and only the seeds remain to pro-duce the next season's generation. These soft-bodied plants are called *herbs,* as opposed to *woody plants* like shrubs and trees.

In this growing cycle the big differences between a buttercup and a sycamore begin. The tree will take many years to become old enough to flower. During all this time it will be spreading a a mass of roots, building a strong woody stem, and extending a crown of leafy branches. The roots, except for their size and woodiness, are much like those of the buttercup. Their purpose is to anchor the plant and to absorb from the earth great

7

quantities of water containing dissolved minerals. Since a full-grown tree has a tremendous top-heavy weight, its underground anchor must spread wide and deep. In some trees the mass of roots is four or five times the size of the crown. Sometimes the roots reach more than a hundred feet down into the earth; sometimes their growth is wide and shallow. The seedling's original tiny rootlet eventually grows enormous, and other roots spread out, branching and rebranching, till those at the very tip are as fine and delicate as a buttercup's. They are covered with minute velvety hairs, able to absorb water through their thin walls.

In the stems that rise above these roots, the differences between tree and buttercup become very obvious, even though both stems perform the same functions. They provide support and at the same time are a system of pipes that carry upward the water and minerals the roots have collected. Then they distribute to all parts of the plant the food manufactured by the leaves. In a tree's stem, or trunk, this becomes a monumental task—drawing up water, against gravity, as much as three hundred feet in the air. The trunk must also hold aloft a heavy mass of leafy branches; it must endure storms and stand intact, sometimes for hundreds of years. So it is designed for strength and durability.

The first green stem of a seedling tree is as soft as that of an herb—a core of pith surrounded by a layer of growing cells and covered by a thin skin. A mature tree has the same construction: a layer of skin, or bark, encloses it from the tip of the highest twig to the end of the deepest rootlet. Inside this skin is the sheath of growing cells, or *cambium*, and then the core of wood. During every growing season, the cells of the cambium multiply by dividing. Old cells on its inner surface develop into *xylem,* or *sapwood,* a layer composed mostly of hollow tubes that carry water upward. Xylem cells live for a few years; then they die, fill up with gums and resins, and become tough solid *heartwood.*

In the same way, the cells on the outer surface of the cambium add each year a new layer inside the bark. This is *phloem,* with channels that carry food to all parts of the tree. Some of its outer cells are corky and waterproof, and these, along with dead phloem cells, make up the bark. As layer after layer is added inside it, the old bark stretches and cracks and finally falls off in scales or fibers.

This is the way a tree grows and keeps on growing throughout the whole of its life. Each season adds a layer of cells to the wood—large open tubes in the spring, and smaller tubes in summer. Thus, when a tree is cut down, a cross section of its trunk clearly shows how many seasons it grew.

The heartwood is the part of a tree used for lumber. The

A TREE'S ANNUAL RINGS

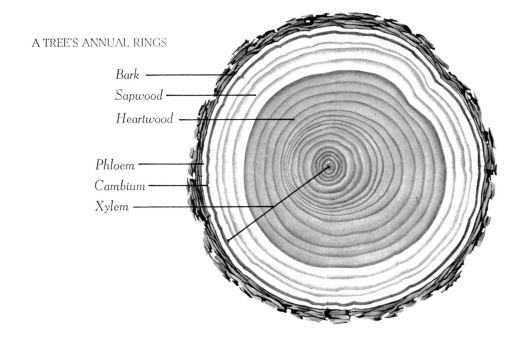

Bark ———

Sapwood ———

Heartwood ———

Phloem ———

Cambium ———

Xylem ———

beautiful grain of woods valued for furniture is the result of the growth rings and other variations in the layers of cells, such as the wavy and irregular patterns produced wherever a limb branches out. Heartwood is so durable that objects made from it can last almost forever. It provides the tree with a support as strong as a granite column, but it is only a support and not essential to the life and growth of the tree. The vital part is the layer of living cells between the bark and the heartwood —the phloem, cambium, and xylem. A tree will die if a ring around the trunk cuts all the way through this layer. But it can live for years with almost all its heartwood gone, its trunk

BLACK WILLOW

RED OAK

PAPER BIRCH

and branches hollowed out by decay or the burrowing of insects or animals.

The thickening of a tree's trunk, branches, and roots is the result of the layers added year after year by the cambium, but lengthwise growth takes place only at the tips of roots and at growing points on the twigs. These growing points are buds, each one containing a miniature shoot, with stem and leaves and sometimes flowers. Each year a tree produces new buds and adds to its size by the length of its new stems, and each year it is crowned anew with a mass of green leaves.

The leaves of a tree serve exactly the same function as the

SUGAR MAPLE

BUTTERNUT

leaves of a buttercup, manufacturing the food that nourishes the entire plant. They are green because their cells contain a green substance called *chlorophyll*. The cells also contain water and minerals that have come up from the roots, and carbon dioxide from the air that has entered through minute pores in the leaf surface. The chlorophyll absorbs energy from the sun and uses the energy to start an intricate chemical process that results in a number of new substances—first sugars, and eventually starches, proteins, and fats. These are food for the plants and, incidentally, for the animals that eat the plants. The chemical process is called *photosynthesis*, and it goes on ceaselessly in every leaf every day, as long as there is light to activate it. The new food products are carried in the phloem to all parts of the tree to be used in growth and production of seeds.

During the chemical activity in the leaves, leftover oxygen and unused water escape as vapor through the leaf pores. These two by-products are tremendously important in the cycle of life on earth. The oxygen sustains all breathing creatures, including man. And the water, drawn by the ton from deep in the earth, provides a large part of the humidity of the atmosphere. A single giant oak can give off three hundred gallons of water a day, or a monthly total of thirty-six tons.

The leaves of most plants, both trees and herbs, are broad and flat, with the greatest possible surface to capture the sun's rays and the air's carbon dioxide. Their chemical activity is greatest in the spring, and by midsummer most of the work of tree leaves is finished. Food has been provided for the year's growth and for the manufacture of flowers and seeds and next year's buds. Gradually the tree progresses toward its winter dormancy. The fresh green is dimmed, the starchmaking is less active, and cells at the base of the leafstalks begin to change. The green chlorophyll in the leaf is slowly withdrawn, and other pigments show themselves. Some of these colors were present all during the life of the leaf, masked by the green; others are new, the products of fall changes. For a few weeks the tree stands clothed in a flame of red or yellow or purple. The cells at every leaf base are by now loose and corky. They loosen its hold on the twig and suddenly the leaf drops, broken off by a breath of air or by its own weight. The layer of cork remains on the twig and becomes a *leaf scar*.

These preparations for winter are another of the big differences between herbs and woody plants. With cold weather, a buttercup dies to the ground; a tree goes into a kind of sleep. In its long life, it passes through cycle after cycle of growth and rest. Tropical trees generally do not change greatly during these alternations. Many of them are evergreen. They grow and rest in response to wet and dry seasons, rather than to warm and cold; and where the climate is very uniform, there are not even growth rings in their trunks. But in cold climates, the *deciduous* trees—the ones that seasonally drop their leaves—become dormant, almost as a hibernating animal does. They then cease to draw water from the earth, to manufacture food, or to grow. Only a faint "breathing" continues: a taking in and giving out of carbon dioxide and oxygen, and a releasing of interior chemical energy. In the absence of leaves, the bark provides a pathway for these gases, through tiny pores in the outer skin of twigs and trunk, which can be seen as little raised dots.

Next summer's leaves and flowers are already formed, wonderfully complete and tightly packaged within the buds. In most trees, each bud is encased in a waterproof wrapping of hard, overlapping scales that are specially modified leaves. The

BLACK CHERRY

WHITE ASH

SHADBUSH

AMERICAN ELM

OHIO BUCKEYE

RED MAPLE

tight covering does not keep the bud warm; it prevents loss of moisture by evaporation, which would kill the tender cells inside. In winter, this stored moisture can freeze solid without damage to the buds, but a freeze can be dangerous after warm temperatures have stirred them to activity. Then cells newly swollen with liquid can be ruptured and killed.

Finally, with spring, the time for reawakening arrives. The air becomes warmer; water flows again and soaks deep into the thawing earth. Tree buds start to grow, nourished by food stored in the roots, the trunk, and the twigs. Each bud swells, and the enclosing scales are pushed open by a tiny shoot of delicate baby leaves. Soon the scales drop off, and the crumpled leaves expand. These first tiny leaflets of spring are very appealing—delicate in texture and color, often pink tinted or softly woolly as a protection from the full glare of the sun. They fill the treetops with a pale green that daily becomes richer and denser. The beauty of all this, and the sense of excitement that comes with each year's unfolding, gives it the quality of a miracle. So the return of life to woods and fields has always been a time for wonder and for man's most joyous festivals.

SPRING BUDS

HICKORY

BUCKEYE

BASSWOOD

ASH

BEECH

MAPLE

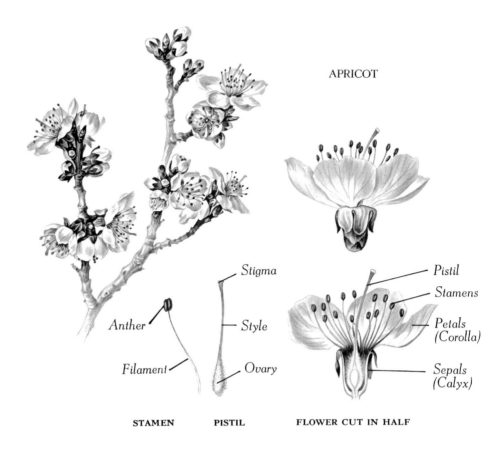

APRICOT

Stigma

Anther

Style

Filament

Ovary

Pistil

Stamens

Petals
(Corolla)

Sepals
(Calyx)

STAMEN　　　**PISTIL**　　　**FLOWER CUT IN HALF**

TREE FLOWERS

The unfolding of leaves, however, is not the earliest event in the spring woods. The very first color that tints the treetops is a pearly haze of pale pinks and yellows and greens. It is so delicate that it often passes quite unnoticed. And when people do notice it, only a few of them have any idea that they are seeing millions of tiny florets hanging on the bare branches overhead. In fact, many people are surprised to learn that trees

16

like oak, elm, and maple have flowers at all. Yet nearly everyone has seen the winged seeds of elm and maple, or is at least familiar with the oak tree's acorns. And seeds like these are produced only by flowers.

Tree flowers, though, are often puzzling on first acquaintance. The sycamore is a flowering plant, and it has the same basic parts that a buttercup has, but its twigs will never bear anything at all resembling a buttercup flower. In fact, its tiny florets, arranged in their tight balls, are quite unlike any familiar "normal" blossom. They are different because they are adapted to a different pollinator—wind instead of insects.

To understand how important this is, one must know how a flower grows and functions. Flowers are the reproductive organs of any plant, whether herb or tree. They bear the male sperm cells and female egg cells; and they exist to produce, nurture, and finally distribute the seeds. An apricot blossom is a typical flower, with its parts arranged in a simple pattern, all clearly visible. In the very center is the vase-shaped *pistil*. It has a knob at the top, called the *stigma*, held up by a stalk, called the *style*. Its round swollen base is the *ovary*, which holds the female *ovules*. Encircling the pistil is a ring of *stamens*, each with a tiny yellow sac (the *anther*) at the end of a thin stalk (the *filament*). The anthers are little bags holding the male *pollen*. Around the stamens is a ring of white *petals*, and then a turned-down ring of green or pinkish *sepals*, which form the *calyx* that originally enclosed and protected the budding flower.

The ovary is destined to become an apricot fruit, but it can never grow into a fruit unless it is *fertilized*. At least one pollen grain must reach the stigma, send a long tube down through the style into the ovary, and there unite its male sperms with

BLACK LOCUST

the female elements of an ovule. Since the stigma of an apricot flower cannot be fertilized by its own anthers, the pollen must come from another apricot flower. This requires the help of some outside agent, usually a honeybee. As bees fly from blossom to blossom gathering nectar and pollen to feed the hive, their furry bodies accidentally pick up a great deal of pollen. It clings as they continue on their rounds, and some of it is inevitably smudged onto the stigma of each flower they visit.

The transfer of pollen from one plant to another of the same species is called *cross-pollination*. In the life and evolution of any species of plant, such crossing is generally an advantage, because it produces a mixture of heredity in the seeds. The offspring will not exactly duplicate either of the parent plants, and new forms will be produced that can meet new conditions. So there is good reason why an apricot flower cannot pollinate itself. Many methods have evolved to bring about this crossbreeding, and most of the methods are illustrated by our tree flowers. But whatever the means of cross-fertilization, some agent has to carry the pollen from flower to flower. These agents are most commonly either insects or wind. Since flowers have been evolving for millions of years in close cooperation with their pollinators, each one now perfectly fits its own particular agent.

The apricot is clearly a flower for insects. Its white petals are visible a long way off. It produces a good store of the nectar and pollen that insects like to eat. Its petals make a good landing place, and a bee or fly of almost any size can easily perch and easily find the nectar.

An elm flower, on the other hand, is obviously not designed for insects. It is extremely small and inconspicuous and not likely to attract the eye of either bee or human. Its struc-

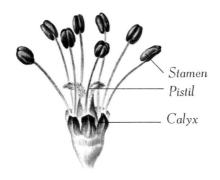

Stamen

Pistil

Calyx

SLIPPERY ELM FLOWER

ture, though quite visible to the naked eye, is much clearer when seen through a magnifying glass. First of all, one notices that it has no petals. Wind-pollinated flowers do not need to provide a foothold or to advertise. Breezes blow whether invited or not, and showy petals could prove a hindrance by keeping air currents from reaching stamens and pistils. So the unnecessary petals, when not completely lacking, are small in size and dull in color—most often, green or greenish yellow.

The prominent parts of an elm flower are the strictly essential parts—the stamens and the pistil. The protruding furry stigma easily catches and holds pollen grains, and most wind-flowers have similar pistils, which stand out boldly with feathery or ruffled stigmas. The stamens of these flowers very often have long filaments like those of the elm, with dangling anthers ready to send off puffs of pollen at the slightest movement. Sometimes, however, as in oak, birch, and walnut, the pollen is shaken out by the swaying of the long flexible catkins of staminate flowers. In any case, great clouds of pollen are

20

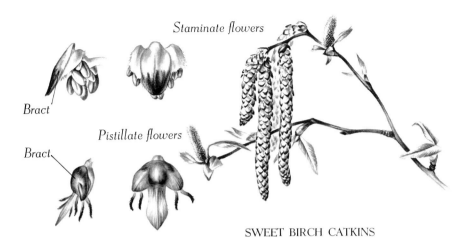

Staminate flowers

Bract

Pistillate flowers

Bract

SWEET BIRCH CATKINS

broadcast—enough to insure that some of it will reach the right pistils in spite of its hit-or-miss distribution. Annoyed housewives often sweep from their patios piles of yellow dust shed by neighboring trees, and smaller pollen showers can be stirred up by anyone who jiggles a cottonwood or birch catkin. The spring air is full of all kinds of pollen, from both trees and grasses, and it causes almost as much hay-fever misery as ragweed pollen does in the fall.

Stamens and pistils are tender, vital parts that need protection from the chills of early spring, and in most tree flowers the sheathing calyx is very important. Sometimes there are additional protective scales, or *bracts,* as in the alder, which blooms along half-frozen streams even before winter is really over. The tiny florets are grouped in twos and threes, tightly covered by their sepals and the leatherlike bracts. The stamens barely push from beneath this shelter to release their pollen, and they rely on the swaying of the catkin to scatter it. Even the fuzzy stigma arms do not reach very far out into the cold.

Flower

Fruits (samaras)

SLIPPERY ELM

They look like the short legs of a turtle projecting from a hard shell.

Alder blooms only a little ahead of a great tide of tree flowers. All trees that are to be pollinated by the wind must bloom early, while branches are still bare or at least before leaves have grown large enough to impede the passage of pollen through the air. Their anthers split when the weather is warm and dry—ideally, on a clear day with a gentle breeze. Too much wind wastes pollen by carrying it away too rapidly; too little allows it to drop without reaching another tree. To protect the pollen from rain damage, the anther pockets close promptly at the first dampness; and to keep it from drying out on its flight through the air, each grain has a hard waxy outer coat.

The elm flower, bearing both pistil and stamens, is bisexual, or *perfect*, but it does not fertilize itself. Its stigma matures and

ALDER

Pistillate flowers

Fruits

Staminate flowers

shrivels before its anthers are ripe. A freshly opened blossom on one tree must be pollinated by older flowers that have opened on other elms a few days earlier. In some tree flowers, the reverse is true: the anthers mature before the stigma. And many trees have an even more positive way of achieving cross-pollination— some of their flowers contain pistils only, while others contain only stamens. This is true of oak, hickory, and alder, which all bear their staminate flowers in hanging mobile catkins. Pistillate flowers nearly always stand up at the ends of twigs, rigid and comparatively still, waiting for pollen to fall on them. Sometimes they grow in small erect catkins, as in alder and birch; sometimes they are borne singly or in small groups, as in oak and hickory. And, as though this separation of the sexes were

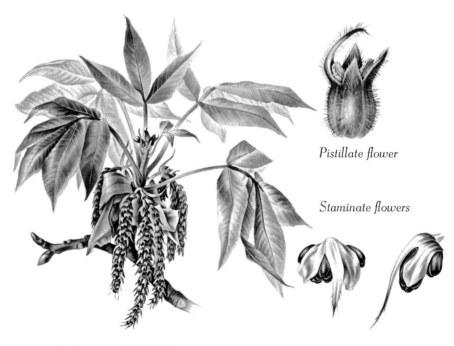

Pistillate flower

Staminate flowers

SHAGBARK HICKORY

not enough, pistils and stamens are sometimes kept even farther apart: in poplars, willows, and ashes, for instance, pistillate and staminate flowers grow on entirely separate trees.

Tiny, inconspicuous flowers are nearly always the mark of a wind-pollinated plant, but there are exceptions to the rule. Some trees, especially maples and willows, are pollinated by insects even though they appear to be perfect windflowers. Possibly in their early history they were wind-pollinated and have changed over to insects in recent times, geologically speaking. Red maple florets, for instance, have only their bright color to suggest their relationship to insects; everything else about them seems designed for the wind—their small size, their pistils and stamens in separate flowers, their habit of

Fruit (nut)

SHAGBARK HICKORY

blooming before the leaves appear. But the flowers secrete nectar and are very popular with bees and flies.

Pussy willow is even more surprising. Pistillate and staminate flowers grow on separate trees, and the decorative "pussies" are the young catkins, with their minute florets still buried inside silvery protective fur. Even when the catkins mature, there appears to be nothing about the florets to interest insects —no petals, no sepals, only tiny bare stamens and pistils sheltered by a small dark scale and a fringe of fine hairs. But that appearance is deceiving. At the base of each floret is a green gland, the source of fragrance and copious nectar, that attracts swarms of insects. Blooming when winter is scarcely past, pussy willows furnish bees with the first honey of the year.

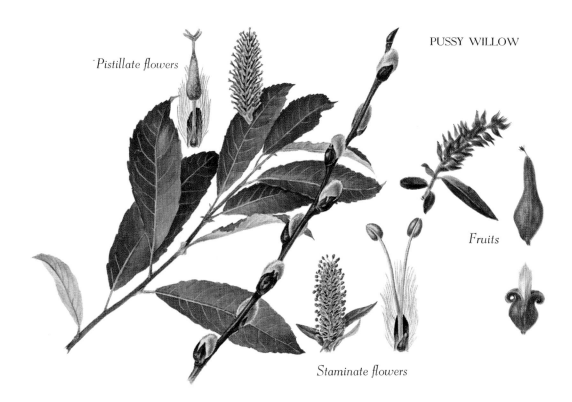

Pistillate flowers

PUSSY WILLOW

Fruits

Staminate flowers

RED MAPLE

Staminate flowers

Pistillate flower

Fruits (samaras)

HAWTHORN

In the forests of North America, the wind-pollinated trees far outnumber the insect-pollinated ones. They are the trees that fill the leafless woods with masses of spring bloom, and they are certainly entitled to be called "flowering trees." Yet all horticulturists quite unfairly reserve that term for the showy ornamentals, which are showy simply because their flowers must be attractive to the insects that pollinate them.

The tulip-tree is a good example of an insect-tree, with its bisexual flowers and its petals large and bright enough to be

28

seen from a distance. The petals of such flowers also provide insects with a good foothold, and they are marked with spots that point the way to the nectar. Pistils and stamens commonly occur in the same blossom, generally maturing at different times to insure cross-fertilization. But sometimes, as in spice-bush and sassafras, the pistillate and staminate flowers are borne on separate trees. The pollen of all insect-flowers tends to be heavy and sticky—suitable for clinging rather than for blowing about.

Though insects and wind are the commonest bearers of tree pollen, they are not the only ones. In tropical forests, where thick foliage prevents wind pollination at any time of year, many nectar-eating birds join the insects as carriers. Hummingbirds are the most numerous and most active of these, and the only ones familiar to Northerners. There are even mammals that pollinate tree flowers, including possums and flying squirrels in Australia and bats in many parts of the world. The big treelike saguaro cactus of Arizona, for instance, is pollinated chiefly by bats, along with doves and a variety of insects.

Trees with pollinizing agents like these do not, of course, need to bloom in the leafless days of early spring. But in most of the United States the procession of blossoms does start early, and some of the small insect-trees, like redbud and spice-bush, add brilliant splashes of color to the bare woods at the same time the wind-flowers are blooming overhead. They are taking advantage of the sun, before the leafy roof closes over them. Flowers of sassafras, shadbush, and dogwood open along with their unfolding leaflets. Other trees, like horse-chestnut and catalpa, wait till their leaves are fully developed, relying on the size or brilliance of their blossoms to attract

TULIP-TREE

BASSWOOD

the attention of insects. Or, like basswood, they tempt the bees with copious nectar and waves of intense fragrance. A few wait till late summer or fall and barely have time to ripen their fruits before cold weather arrives. And witch-hazel comes last of all, flashing yellow in bare November woods in a kind of reversal of spring. The flowers remind one of forsythia, and they provide the very last forage for late-working bees. But this tardiness delays for a whole year the production of witch-hazel seeds—they will not be fully ripened until the following autumn.

APRICOT

Ovule

Seed

FRUIT CUT IN HALF

FRUITS

Everyone knows that apples and pears and oranges are borne on "fruit trees." But "fruit tree" is another artificial and misleading term, because all flowering trees are fruiting trees. Used accurately, the word *fruit* means any structure that holds the seeds of a plant. It may be plump and tasty, like that of the apricot, or hard and dry, like that of the elm. Basically it is a flower's ripened ovary, with the ripened ovules (seeds) inside. But sometimes other parts of the flower grow along with the ovary to form part of the fruit.

A fruit starts to develop the moment a flower is fertilized. As soon as a pollen tube has entered an ovule and released its minute sperm cells, a new plant begins to grow. Each fertilized ovule contains one of these young plants—called an *embryo*—and becomes one seed. In general, only fertilization can start this growth, but there are some fruits that can develop without it.

In an apricot, which has a fairly simple arrangement of parts, the growth from ovary to fruit is easy to understand. The sweet, juicy part of the ripe fruit is the body of the ovary grown large and succulent. The ovary's inner wall has become a very hard protective shell that surrounds the seed. The seed itself has only a thin brown skin, and inside it is the embryo plant surrounded by a considerable amount of food. The food —starch and protein and oil—will sustain the infant plant until it has sprouted and grown large enough to spread its own green leaves.

Normally, only one of the apricot flower's two ovules develops into a seed. But occasionally both ovules develop and produce the same kind of double kernel that is sometimes found in an almond. An almond "nut" is constructed in exactly the same way as an apricot pit, because the two trees are closely related. In one case, we eat the fleshy body of the ovary; in the other case, the seed.

In becoming a fruit, the apricot ovary changes a great deal in size as well as in texture. But a grapefruit is the result of even greater change, and so is a coconut. Any seed, whether the size of a coconut or the size of a grain of sand, is simply an embryo plant enclosed in a protective wrapping along with a large or small amount of food. When the food supply is very small, the seeds have to grow quickly after germination or die.

All true nuts are fruits; and so are the hanging pods of the locusts and redbuds (called *legumes* by botanists); the winged *samaras* of maple, elm, and ash; the *drupes* of peach, mango, and olive; and the *berries* of persimmon and papaya. These names indicate various kinds of fruit structure. But all fruits have one common purpose: they protect the ripening seeds and help to distribute them. Sometimes this distribution is quite literal and dramatic, as when witch-hazel pods suddenly snap open and shoot their seeds in all directions. More often the

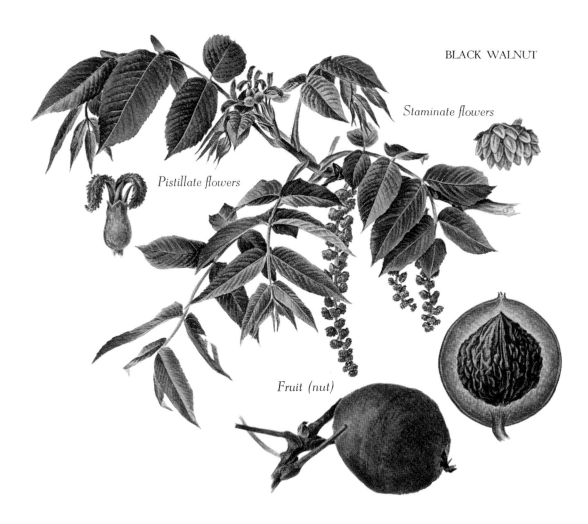

BLACK WALNUT

Staminate flowers

Pistillate flowers

Fruit (nut)

WITCH-HAZEL

job is done by wind or animals. All the winged and plumed
seeds are carried by the wind, and they are distributed all
around us by the millions every summer. On an elm-lined
city street, one tramps over a carpet of samaras. The long-
haired seeds of poplar and willow fill the air with flying
"cotton," and sometimes clog screens and drains. Ailanthus
has become a weed in the city because its seeds fly everywhere
and are able to root in any handful of dust. Nuts and acorns
are carried off and buried by squirrels, and many of them
sprout and grow before they can be eaten. Even when fruits
are eaten by birds and mammals and people, the seeds usually

35

find their way back to the earth. Some are simply thrown aside, and others can pass unharmed through an animal's digestive system.

Seeds float in brooks and rivers. Coconuts often drop into the ocean, to be washed up on some distant beach where the new plant sprouts in the barren sand, nourished by the immense amount of food stored inside the shell. Red mangrove trees, which always grow in shallow water, have fruits with the curious habit of sprouting while still hanging on the branches. They grow a tough, spikelike root, and when they become too heavy, they drop straight down into the mud, and another mangrove is planted.

The seeds of such trees as willow and birch, inside their winged fruits, are not much bigger than the head of a pin. The seeds of maple, ash, and elm, without their wings, are a little larger—perhaps a quarter inch in length—but even so they do not seem able to hold the beginnings of a hundred-foot tree. However, the size of the seed, or of the embryo inside it, has nothing to do with the eventual size of the plant that will grow from it. Every new plant, as well as every animal, starts from a single fertilized cell. The cells multiply by dividing and redividing, and if the sequence goes on for two or three hundred years, with old cells not falling away when they die, the resulting edifice of cells will be very large indeed.

Plants, unlike most animals, can reproduce themselves in other ways than by fertilized cells. Young trees often follow old ones by the sprouting of old stumps, the young trees richly nourished by the large root system of the parent. Sometimes the roots of living trees send up these "suckers," and the old tree grows on, surrounded by a grove of saplings. Willows freely drop their brittle twigs, which take root in the earth and grow; and the twigs of many other trees will do the same thing, though not so easily as the willows do. These methods of growing plants are called *vegetative* reproduction. They are of special importance to gardeners, who produce new trees by rooting small pieces cut from valuable varieties or by grafting them to the branches of tougher but less valuable trees. This can cause some surprising effects—like a white-blossoming hawthorn tree with a single branch of pink flowers.

In nature, vegetative reproduction is added to seed making as one more way of assuring the survival of a species. But a plant grown from a seed is a new creation, a mixture of the substance of two separate parents. A plant grown by vegetative means is not truly a new plant; it is merely an extension of an old one.

BLACK GUM

Pistillate flowers

Staminate flowers

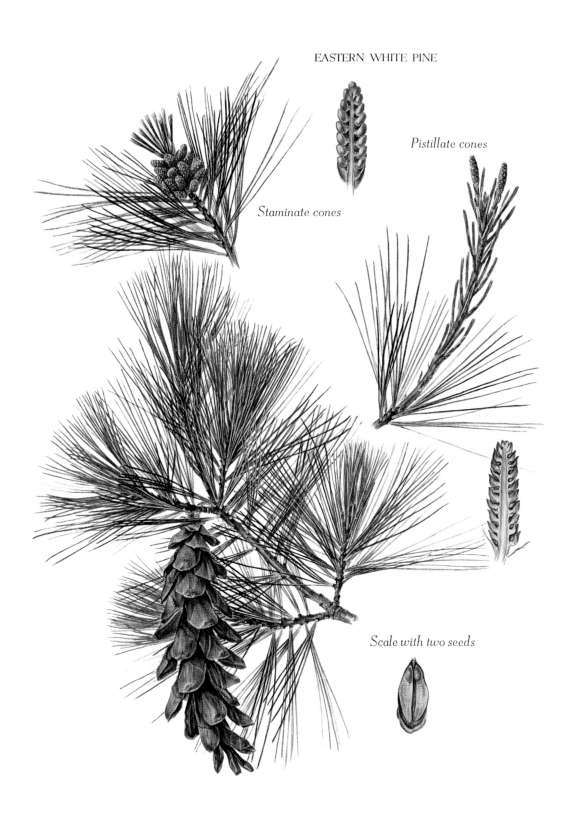

EASTERN WHITE PINE

Pistillate cones

Staminate cones

Scale with two seeds

GYMNOSPERMS

The scientific name for the trees commonly called ever-greens or conifers is *gymnosperm*. This word comes from two Greek words meaning "naked seed," because the seeds of these plants are not enclosed in an ovary as are those of true flower-ing plants, which are called *angiosperms*. Pines, spruces, firs, cedars—all these are gymnosperms. Most gymnosperms are evergreen, but some, like the tamarack, shed their leaves in winter. Even the evergreen leaves eventually fall, but they sometimes cling for a very long time—as much as seventeen years in a bristlecone pine. Most gymnosperms bear their seeds in cones, but some do not: the seeds of yew grow in bright red berrylike cups. And most have needle-shaped or scale-shaped leaves, though some, like the ginkgo, do not. Their method of fertilizing ovules and producing seeds is practically the same as that of flowering trees, and only structural differences keep their reproductive organs from being called flowers. In fact, even botanists sometimes call them flowers, for lack of a better name.

In white pine, as in most gymnosperms, male and female cells are produced by separate "flowers" on the same tree. The pollen-bearing stamens, with fat anthers and almost no fila-ments, are densely massed on a central core, the anthers ex-posed like those of a willow catkin. When ripe, the bright yellow anthers split open to let out an enormous amount of pollen. It is carried by the wind in a yellow cloud—enough to fall on every ovule and still pile up in little drifts on the ground.

The female cells grow in small conelike structures, with many ovule-bearing scales attached to the central core. Purple-tinted or sometimes red, the pretty little clusters are rarely seen, because they usually grow only on the topmost branches of the large pine trees, one or two at the tip of each twig. After pollen has reached their bare ovules, the little cones grow and toughen, and at the end of their first season they have become tight bullet-shaped bodies about an inch long. By the end of the second season, their seeds are mature, and their scales are hard and woody. Slim and fingerlike, they hang from the upper branches for a few more months, till the scales are dry enough to curl back and release the winged seeds to the wind.

Conifers are most abundant in cold and temperate regions. They are called ''softwoods'' in contrast with the ''hardwood'' deciduous trees, but this distinction is not very accurate. They provide 75 percent of the world's timber and nearly all the pulp used for paper. And they include the world's largest and oldest trees. Sequoias can grow as tall as 380 feet, with trunks 30 feet in diameter, and Douglas-firs are nearly as tall. Some sequoias are estimated to be four thousand years old; one huge

ARBORVITAE   CYPRESS

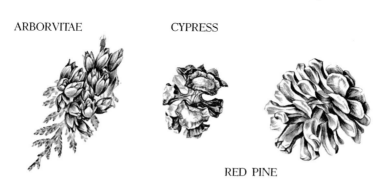

RED PINE

Mexican cypress is probably still older, and a certain bristlecone pine in California is thought to be about forty-six hundred.

Gymnosperms developed on the earth much earlier than flowering trees—about three hundred million years ago, following the giant ferns of the Coal Age. They differed from the ferns, with seeds instead of spores and strong wood instead of fibrous trunks, and over most of the world they replaced the fern forests. They were all pollinated primarily by the wind. But they may also have been the earliest plants to receive pollen from insects, because beetles, which ate the tender cones and the pollen itself, probably carried some of it from tree to tree.

Eventually a new kind of tree evolved to compete with the gymnosperms: the flowering plant, with seeds enclosed in protective ovaries, complex flowers adapted to all kinds of new pollinizing agents, and leaves that were dropped and renewed each year. These new trees were more complicated and more varied, and as the earth changed through geologic time, they evolved to fit a great variety of landscapes and climates. But the conifers were not displaced. They still dominate great areas of the earth and mingle with the flowering trees in other places.

PINYON   HEMLOCK

BLUE SPRUCE

YEW

FOREST REGIONS

At the time when the continents of the earth finally settled into the shape they bear today, the mantle of green that had been displaced by the rising and falling of mountains and the coming and going of glaciers began to spread over the earth again. In each region there evolved an interrelated group of plants and animals suited to living together in that environment. The continent of North America, reaching from the frozen Arctic to the Tropics, includes almost every possible variation of land and climate, and a great part of this variety lies within the United States. The groups of plants that inhabit each small section are, of course, varied too. But in general, the forest land falls into a large simple pattern governed by temperature and the presence of water.

The great Northeastern Forest occupies a region that extends from the Mississippi River to the Atlantic Ocean. It

HORSE-CHESTNUT

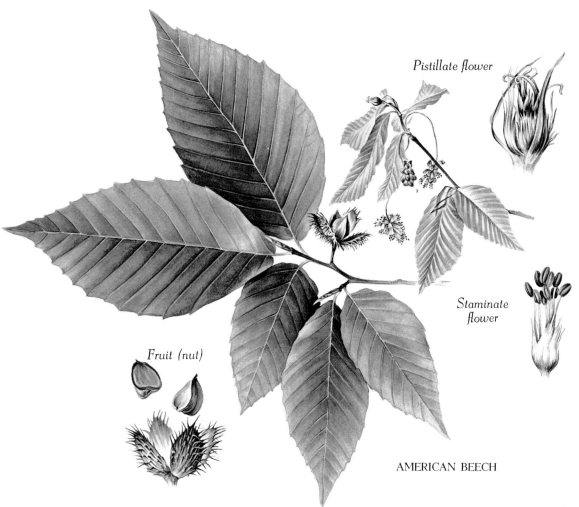

Pistillate flower

Staminate flower

Fruit (nut)

AMERICAN BEECH

blends into the Canadian Conifer Forest to the north and stretches southward till it is replaced by the Southern Forest. West of the Mississippi is the almost treeless region of the Great Plains. The Rocky Mountains can be considered either a region by themselves or a part of the Northwestern Forest. The Southwestern Desert, from California to Texas, is another region. These are the important forest areas, but one might also list the state of California, with its many exceptional trees, and a tiny area at the tip of Florida that is pure Tropics.

44

The Northeastern United States is one of the few parts of the world naturally covered by great deciduous forests. Parts of Northern Europe once had similar woodlands, but centuries of civilization there have nearly wiped them out, as land has been cleared for agriculture and trees cut for lumber. When the first colonists from Europe arrived on our Eastern shore, they found an almost unbroken band of trees extending from Canada to Florida. From the coast, it reached inland so far that they did not fully explore its depths for several generations. It was, and still is, a magnificent hardwood forest with an intermingling of conifers. Though much smaller now, it has not yet been destroyed, and more than three hundred species of trees still grow wild in it.

A forest of this sort probably offers more beauty and delight than any other kind. It certainly offers more variety, in the progression of its yearly changes. In earliest spring there is the pearly cloud of wind-pollinated flowers, soon replaced by a bright green cloud of tiny new leaves. The heat of summer is tempered by a canopy of richer green, periodically broken by the handsome flowers of insect-pollinated trees. All this ends in the dramatic fireworks of autumn, an arboreal event unequaled anywhere in the world. In winter the beauty is more subtle—a lacework of trunks and branches against the sky, the shape and texture of bare twigs, the charm of leaf scars and snug winter buds.

Much of the beauty of the Northeastern Forest results from the mixture of many kinds of trees, and so does much of its strength. Great epidemics can wipe out one species of tree, as they destroyed the chestnut and may yet destroy the American elm, but other kinds will survive.

In a full-grown forest, there is tremendous competition for growing space and light. The big trees grow tall and straight as they reach toward the sun, and their lower branches die and drop off. (In an open field they may be quite different in shape—well rounded, with branches almost to the ground.) Under the big trees, there are little trees. Some are very young, a new generation growing from dropped seeds; others are *understory* trees, often more like shrubs. But they do not branch at ground level as shrubs do, and their slender crooked

SASSAFRAS

Pistillate flower

Staminate flowers

trunks often bend and twist as they spread their growth toward the nearest patch of sunlight. Many of them, like dogwood, shadbush, and redbud, have beautiful flowers, and they also have the charm of being within easy reach. One can touch the bark and examine the leaves and winter buds, an intimacy not always possible with large trees.

Of the trees in the Northeastern Forest, about fifteen can be considered especially important—beautiful in outline and detail, impressive in size, valuable for timber, plentiful in a wide area. They are marked with two stars in the list at the end of this book. Many of these fine trees have been brought into

SHADBUSH

cultivation and are widely planted in parks and on city streets. An elm-bordered road may be the trademark of a New England village, but Northeastern elms and oaks and maples will grow in almost any part of the United States, so long as the climate is not too hot or too cold and water is plentifully supplied by nature or by man.

But some of our best-loved garden trees are immigrants from Europe or Asia or Australia. Many of them came to this country with the early colonists; others were brought in more recently by horticulturists. Horse-chestnut and weeping willow both originated in Asia; and so did the ailanthus, or tree-of-heaven, which found the United States so much to its liking that it has become a weed in some parts of the country. Most orchard trees are here only because they were brought long ago by settlers from Europe. We do have a number of native wild cherries and plums and crab apples, but the trees that bear fruit grown for market are descendants of trees that originated in Europe or Asia and have been in cultivation for thousands of years.

Most imported species, however, are common only in parks and gardens and orchards; none but the toughest of newcomers can find a place in the well-established forests. So the weeping willow never competes with the forty or so species of American willows. And the beautiful European and Asian lindens grow only along streets and in parks, not in the woods where we find the American linden, or basswood.

In the Northeastern Forest, many conifers mingle with the hardwoods, and they increase in number as one moves northward. Finally the conifers take over and completely dominate the woods of Canada.

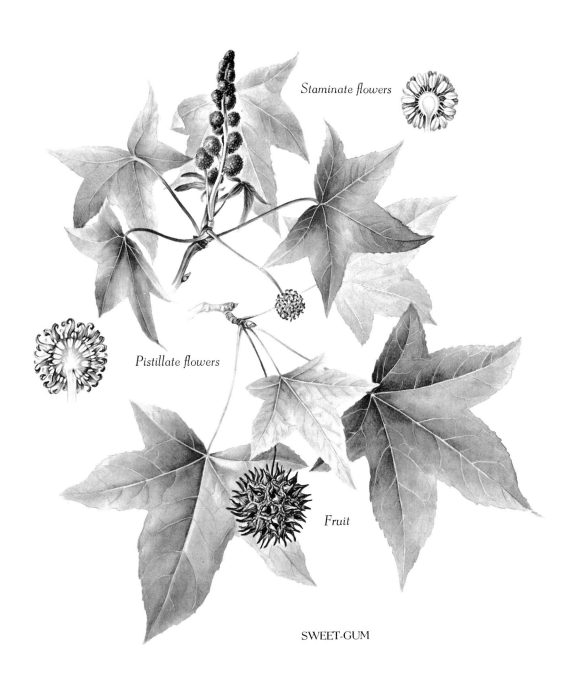

Staminate flowers

Pistillate flowers

Fruit

SWEET-GUM

THE SOUTHERN FOREST

Southward, too, the woods change gradually. Perhaps the Southern Forest may be said to start at that irregular line where the live oaks first appear. These great spreading evergreen trees, with their festoons of Spanish moss, are truly and typically Southern. But many of the commonest Northern trees —oaks and elms and maples—grow widely in the South; and others, like sweet-gum, honeylocust, and persimmon, may be considered as Southern trees that grow widely in the North. In this warm region, many trees besides conifers are evergreen, and many have large handsome flowers. The big-flowered magnolia is one of the most beautiful, with its creamy white

50

BIG-FLOWER MAGNOLIA

blossoms and glossy dark foliage. The cabbage palmetto, a palm with fan-shaped leaves, is another tree that seems to typify the South; but it should, more accurately, typify only Florida since it is common only in that state.

The South has the largest pine forest in the world. It spreads from Washington, D.C., to Florida and around the Gulf Coast to Texas. Scattered through it are great swamps where the bald cypress grows. These strange trees are found nowhere else in the world, and like the live oaks, they are symbols of the South. Stately forests of bald cypress rise a hundred feet tall out of the water and mud. Their trunks flare at the base to give them better anchorage, and all around them gnarled stumps, called "knees," rise above the water. These are roots which cannot find enough oxygen under water and, quite literally, have come up for air.

In the South, the changing of leaves is a gradual and individual matter. Even the deciduous trees do not end their growing period with a unanimous celebration of color, and there is little to mark outwardly the rhythm of the seasons.

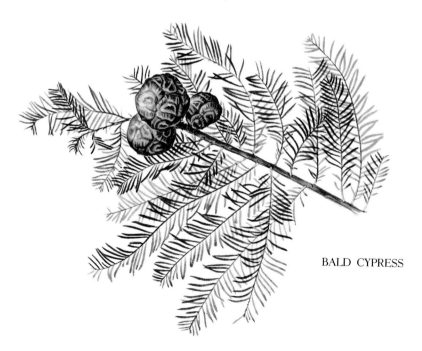

BALD CYPRESS

BOX-ELDER

THE GREAT PLAINS

The central part of the United States, rising gradually from the Mississippi River to the Rocky Mountains, is a vast grassy plain that becomes drier as it progresses westward. At the farthest edge, there is enough rain to support a rich variety of grasses and other herbaceous plants, but not enough for trees; they grow only in narrow ribbons along the streams that wind across the prairies—mostly cottonwoods, along with a few willows and small maples. Moving eastward, one finds more trees: groves of bur oak, box-elder, and Osage-orange, growing with a carpet of grass beneath them, rather than an understory

53

of bushes. Still farther east, trees of the Northeastern and Southern forests begin to appear, and gradually the three regions blend imperceptibly together.

In fact, many Northeastern trees can be found scattered throughout this dry land. Easterners who settled there were homesick for the green woods they had left behind; around their towns and homesteads, they planted familiar trees and then worked heroically to keep them alive with irrigation.

PLAINS COTTONWOOD

Fruits

Pistillate flowers

Staminate flowers

DOUGLAS-FIR

THE NORTHWESTERN FOREST

The tree world of the Northwest is utterly different from any other part of the United States. It is a world of steep mountains and deep valleys, richly watered by moist winds from the Pacific Ocean. Trees here grow to gigantic size, so tall and straight that their tops are lost to sight. They are nearly all conifers, with dense blue-green foliage that looks almost black against the sky and makes the understory into a dark, silent world. These forests seem completely timeless; they are majestic and awe-inspiring and without the infinite variety of Eastern woods. They have comparatively few kinds of trees: Douglas-fir, pine, true fir, spruce, cedar, with small patches of deciduous trees winding down through the valleys.

These great forests follow the Sierra Nevada Mountains down into California, and similar conifer forests clothe the Rockies from Canada to New Mexico. But the Rockies lack the wet ocean winds; many coast species cannot live there, and other species, like Douglas-fir and ponderosa pine, grow only half as large as they do in Oregon.

55

Forests of this sort change little from season to season. But against the constant dark green of the conifers, the deciduous trees set minor patterns with their light summer greens and autumn reds and yellows. In the Rockies, it is the quaking aspen, almost alone, that spreads masses of intense color among the evergreens when its twinkling "silver-dollar" leaves turn to gold in the fall. The aspen is the one tree that grows naturally all across the United States, from Maine to California. It quakes because its leaves, like those of most poplars, are attached to the twigs with a little twist, so that they tremble in the slightest breath of air.

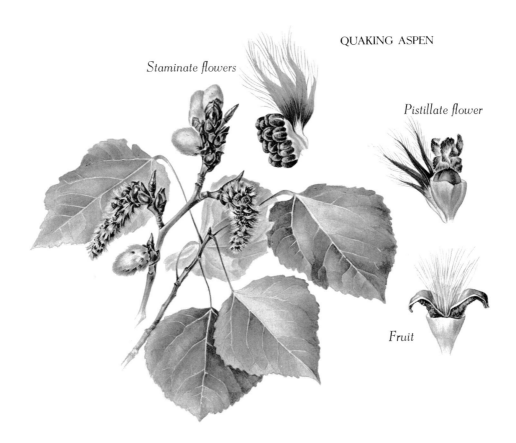

QUAKING ASPEN

Staminate flowers

Pistillate flower

Fruit

SAGUARO CACTUS

THE SOUTHWESTERN DESERT

In the Southwestern United States there are a few spots with no water at all—alkali flats or barren, shifting sands where no vegetation of any kind exists. But most of the Southwestern American Desert receives some moisture, and it supports a surprising number of plants. They are all very different from "normal" plants, with structure or habits adapted to their special kind of life. Much of this life is spent in a dormancy rather like the winter sleep of Northern trees, and only after the brief spring rains does the whole desert awake with a feverish rush of flowers. There is so little water that few of these plants grow very large, and not many could be called trees. The giant organ-pipe cactus or saguaro, however, grows

57

as tall as fifty feet. Its thick succulent stems store water, and its tiny scalelike leaves last only a short time and then leave the manufacture of food to the green stems. Each of its beautiful white flowers opens for a single day.

The Joshua-tree is a strange-looking member of the Lily family, a fantasy of angular branches and clumps of sharp, swordlike leaves. Blue paloverde is much more normal in appearance, a beautiful little tree during the brief rainy season. At that time it has plenty of blue-green leaves and a mass of yellow flowers; but with the end of the rain, it drops all the leaves, so they will not be giving off precious water during the hot summer. The bright green trunk and branches then take over the food-making for the plant.

The Southwest is not a region of forests, and these trees of the hot desert are unlike trees anywhere else. Some seem like plants from a different planet.

BLUE PALOVERDE

EUCALYPTUS

Flower cut in half

Fruit cut in half

REDWOOD

CALIFORNIA

California is a region of exceptions. The state stretches six hundred miles from north to south and rises from below sea level in Death Valley to fourteen thousand feet in the high mountains. The inland mountains—the Sierra Nevadas—are covered by an extension of the Northwestern Conifer Forest, but they have one spectacular addition—the giant sequoias. Some of these mighty trees, standing there for three thousand years, have piled up twelve million pounds of growth and built a trunk thirty-five feet thick. They seem not in the scale of living things, but like part of the mountain itself.

California's other great sequoia is the redwood that grows near the coast. It is the world's tallest tree, and to sustain its great bulk, it must have fifty to sixty inches of rain a year, in addition to ocean fog every night. This it finds only in a limited area of northern California. The sequoias have a high resistance to fire, insects, and disease, and only recently has

60

there appeared an enemy able to destroy them—the lumberman with a power-driven saw.

Other rare trees grow along this unique coastline, plentiful in one small area and nowhere else on earth: Monterey cypress, Oregon myrtle, madrone, and a few others. On the other hand, the trees in California's hot central valley have been gathered from all over the world—the cultivated citrus and olives, the figs and palms and eucalyptus. Eucalyptus is the most conspicuous tree in the inhabited parts of the state. There are several species, all brought from Australia, and all able to thrive in rainless hot climates. Their roots travel deep for water, and in hot weather the slender leaves curl lengthwise and turn their edges toward the sun, thus reducing evaporation from their flat surfaces.

Southern California is warm enough for many tropical trees, but it is too dry for them to grow without cultivation.

TROPICAL FLORIDA

The southern tip of Florida is a tiny piece of the real Tropics. It is warm enough and wet enough to be hospitable to the same plants that grow on the islands and southern shores of the Caribbean, and also to many trees brought from other parts of the world, like the showy royal poinciana. Most of them are evergreen, and they have large and often dramatic blossoms. In these jungles, the competition is intense, and only conspicuous flowers are likely to be seen and visited by pollinators.

But, beautiful as such trees are, they seem alien—not really a part of any American forest.

REDBUD

LOOK UP TO THE TREES

Trees represent a great many different plant families. Some of these families—like Maple, Oak, and Birch—include only trees; but others include herbs and vines as well, since plant relationships depend on flowers and fruits rather than on size and manner of growth. Trees are often cousins of familiar garden plants, and no one should be surprised to learn, for instance, that redbud and locust trees belong to the same family as string beans and wisteria. All these flowers have the same "butterfly" construction, and all produce the same kind of seed pods. The Rose family includes both hybrid tea roses and the trees that produce nearly all our Northern fruits —apples, cherries, plums, apricots, and many others. And the little woodland violet belongs to a family that contains thirteen kinds of tropical trees.

But in spite of all these close relationships, the flowers of the treetops are inevitably less familiar than flowers that grow in a garden border or beside a country path. Small plants at our feet are always easier to see and know than the large ones that bend over us like a kind of architecture. We are inclined to take this architecture for granted—to regard it as a framework or background for our lives, not to be touched and examined or enjoyed in intimate detail. But a tree is not mere architecture. It is a living organism, constantly changing; and only by touching and examining it can we learn the intricacy and beauty of its life cycle.

This is not an easy intimacy. Very few trees carry their flowers and fruits, or even their leaves, at the eye level of a man. But the special joy of holding in one's hand a fluffy sprig of maple flowers, a drooping cluster of ash samaras, or a sleek twig of winter beech is worth the considerable effort it often takes to find them. And familiarity will not in any way diminish our respect and reverence for these most majestic and enduring of living things.

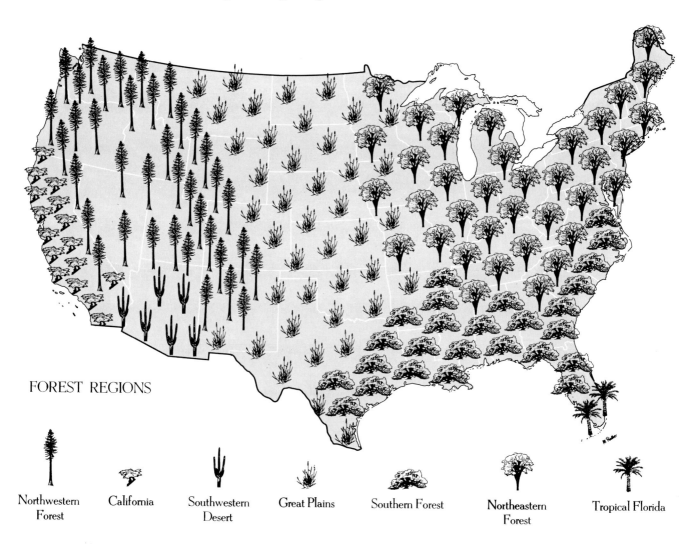

FOREST REGIONS

Northwestern Forest   California   Southwestern Desert   Great Plains   Southern Forest   Northeastern Forest   Tropical Florida

LISTS OF COMMON TREES FOUND IN VARIOUS FOREST REGIONS OF THE UNITED STATES

Especially important trees are marked with two stars; these are beautiful in whole or in part, impressive in size, valuable for timber, and plentiful in a wide area. A group somewhat less important, but outstanding, is marked with one star. The authority for all Latin and common names used in this book is *Wyman's Garden Encyclopedia*, edited by Diane Harris.

THE NORTHEASTERN FOREST

Abies balsamea: balsam fir

Acer japonicum: fullmoon maple

Acer nigrum: black maple

*Acer pennsylvanicum: striped maple, moosewood

Acer platanoides: Norway maple

Acer pseudoplatanus: sycamore maple

*Acer rubrum: red maple, swamp maple

Acer saccharinum: silver maple

**Acer saccharum: sugar maple

Acer spicatum: mountain maple

Aesculus glabra: Ohio buckeye

Aesculus hippocastanum: horse-chestnut

Ailanthus altissima: tree-of-heaven

Amelanchier spp.: shadbush, shadblow

Aralia spinosa: Devil's walking stick, Hercules' club

Betula lenta: sweet birch, black birch

*Betula lutea: yellow birch

**Betula papyrifera: paper birch, canoe birch

Betula populifolia: gray birch

Broussonetia papyrifera: common paper-mulberry

Carpinus caroliniana: American hornbeam, ironwood

Carya cordiformis: bitternut

Carya glabra: pignut

Carya illinoensis: pecan

Carya laciniosa: shellbark hickory

**Carya ovata: shagbark hickory

Carya tomentosa: mockernut

Castanea dentata: American chestnut

Catalpa bignonioides: Southern catalpa

Celtis occidentalis: common hackberry

*Cercis canadensis: redbud

Chionanthus virginicus: fringetree

Cladrastis lutea: American yellow-wood

*Cornus florida: flowering dogwood

Crataegus crus-galli: hawthorn, cockspur thorn

Crataegus intricata: thicket hawthorn

Crataegus oxyacantha: English hawthorn

Crataegus phaenopyrum: Washington hawthorn

**Fagus grandifolia: American beech

Fagus sylvatica var. atropunicea: purple beech

**Fraxinus americana: white ash

Fraxinus nigra: black ash

Fraxinus pennsylvanica: red ash

Fraxinus pennsylvanica lanceolata: green ash

Fraxinus quadrangulata: blue ash

Ginkgo biloba: ginkgo

Gleditsia triacanthos: honeylocust

Halesia carolina: Carolina silverbell

*Hamamelis virginiana: common witch-hazel

*Juglans cinerea: butternut

**Juglans nigra: eastern black walnut

Juniperus virginiana: eastern red-cedar

Larix laricina: American larch, tamarack

*Liriodendron tulipifera: tulip-tree

Malus coronaria: crab apple

*Malus pumila: apple

Morus alba: white mulberry

Morus rubra: red mulberry

Ostrya virginiana: hop-hornbeam, ironwood

Paulownia tomentosa: royal paulownia, empress-tree

Picea abies: Norway spruce

Picea glauca: white spruce

Picea mariana: black spruce

Picea rubens: red spruce

Pinus banksiana: jack pine

Pinus resinosa: red pine

Pinus rigida: pitch pine

**Pinus strobus: eastern white pine

Pinus sylvestris: Scotch pine

Pinus virginiana: scrub pine

Platanus acerifolia: London plane-tree

**Platanus occidentalis: American plane-tree, sycamore

Populus alba: white poplar

**Populus deltoides: cottonwood

Populus grandidentata: large-toothed aspen

Populus nigra var. italica: Lombardy poplar

Populus tacamahaca: balsam poplar

**Populus tremuloides: quaking aspen

Prunus avium: mazzard cherry

THE NORTHEASTERN FOREST (*continued*)

Prunus pensylvanica: pin cherry,
  wild red cherry
**Prunus serotina:* black cherry,
  rum cherry
Prunus virginiana: choke-cherry
***Quercus alba:* white oak
Quercus bicolor: swamp white oak
Quercus coccinea: scarlet oak
Querus ilicifolia: scrub oak
Quercus palustris: pin oak
Quercus prinus: chestnut oak
Quercus rubra: red oak

Quercus stellata: post oak
Quercus velutina: black oak
Rhus typhina: staghorn sumac
Rhus vernix: poison sumac
***Robinia pseudoacacia:* black locust
Salix babylonica: weeping willow
Salix discolor: pussy willow
***Salix nigra:* black willow
 **Sassafras albidum:* sassafras
Sorbus americana: American
  mountain-ash
Sorbus aucuparia: European

  mountain-ash
Thuja occidentalis: American arborvitae
***Tilia americana:* basswood,
  American linden
Tilia europea: common linden
Tsuga canadensis: Canada hemlock
***Ulmus americana:* American elm
Ulmus pumila: Siberian elm
Ulmus rubra: slippery elm
Ulmus thomasii: rock elm

THE SOUTHERN FOREST

Betula nigra: river birch
Castanea pumila: Allegany chinkapin
Diospyros virginiana: common
  persimmon
Ilex opaca: American holly
Ilex vomitoria: yaupon
Lagerstroemia indica: crape-myrtle
**Liquidambar styraciflua:* sweet-gum
Magnolia acuminata: cucumber-tree
**Magnolia grandiflora:* southern
  magnolia, big-flower magnolia

Magnolia macrophylla: bigleaf magnolia
Magnolia tripetala: umbrella magnolia
Magnolia virginiana: sweet bay
  magnolia
**Nyssa sylvatica:* black gum, tupelo
Pinus caribaea: slash pine
Pinus echinata: shortleaf pine
**Pinus palustris:* longleaf pine
Pinus taeda: loblolly pine, old field pine
Quercus falcata: Spanish oak
Quercus imbricaria: shingle oak

Quercus laurifolia: laurel oak
Quercus lyrata: overcup oak
Quercus marilandica: blackjack oak
Quercus nigra: water oak
Quercus phellos: willow oak
**Quercus virginiana:* live oak
**Sabal palmetto:* cabbage palmetto
**Taxodium distichum:* bald cypress
Ulmus alata: winged elm
Zanthoxylum clava-herculis:
  southern prickly ash

THE GREAT PLAINS

**Acer negundo:* box-elder
Asimina triloba: papaw
Euonymus atropurpureus:
  eastern wahoo

Gymnocladus dioicus: Kentucky
  coffee-tree
Maclura pomifera: Osage-orange
Oxydendrum arboreum: sorrel-tree,

  sourwood
**Populus sargentii:* plains cottonwood
Ptelea trifolia: hoptree, wafer ash
**Quercus macrocarpa:* bur oak

THE NORTHWESTERN FOREST

Abies amabilis: Cascade fir
Abies concolor: white fir
Abies grandis: grand fir
Abies lasiocarpa: alpine fir
Abies lasiocarpa var. arizonica:
   corkbark fir
Abies magnifica: red fir
Abies procera: noble fir
Acer circinatum: vine maple
Acer macrophyllum: bigleaf maple
Alnus rhombifolia: white alder
Alnus rubra: red alder
Arbutus menziesii: Pacific madrone
Calocedrus decurrens: California
   incense-cedar
Castanopsis chrysophylla: giant
   evergreen-chinkapin
Chamaecyparis lawsoniana: Lawson
   false cypress, Port Orford cedar

Chamaecyparis nootkatensis: Nootka
   false cypress, Alaska cedar
Cornus nuttallii: Pacific dogwood
Fraxinus latifolia: Oregon ash
Juniperus occidentalis: western juniper
Larix occidentalis: western larch
Lithocarpus densiflora: tanbark oak
Picea breweriana: Brewer spruce
Picea engelmannii: Engelmann spruce
Picea pungens: blue spruce,
   Colorado spruce
Picea sitchensis: Sitka spruce
Pinus albicaulis: whitebark pine
Pinus attenuata: knobcone pine
Pinus contorta: shore pine,
   lodgepole pine
Pinus flexilis: limber pine
Pinus jeffreyi: Jeffrey pine
Pinus lambertiana: sugar pine

Pinus monticola: western white pine
Pinus ponderosa: ponderosa pine
Pinus sabiniana: digger pine
Populus trichocarpa: black cottonwood
Pseudotsuga menziesii: Douglas-fir
Quercus chrysolepsis: canyon live oak
Quercus garryana: Oregon white oak
Quercus kelloggii: California black oak
Rhamnus purshiana: cascara buckthorn
Salix spp.: Pacific willow and others
Taxus brevifolia: Pacific yew
Thuja plicata: giant arborvitae,
   western red cedar
Tsuga heterophylla: western hemlock
Tsuga mertensiana: mountain hemlock
Umbellularia californica: California
   laurel, Oregon myrtle

THE SOUTHWESTERN DESERT

Canotia holacantha: crucifixion thorn
Carnegiea gigantea: giant cactus,
   saguaro

Cercidium floridum: blue paloverde
Olneya tesota: desert ironwood
Pinus edulis: pinyon, nut pine

Pinus monophylla: one leaf pinyon
Prosopis juliflora: honey mesquite
Yucca brevifolia: Joshua-tree

CALIFORNIA

Acacia decurrens dealbata: silver wattle
Aesculus californica: California buckeye
Archontophoenix cunninghamiana:
   Seaforthia palm
Arecastrum romanzoffianum: queen palm
Ceratonia siliqua: carob, St. John's bread

Citrus limonia: lemon
Citrus sinensis: orange
Cupressus macrocarpa: Monterey cypress
Eucalyptus camaldulensis: red gum
Eucalyptus citriodora: lemon-scented gum
Eucalyptus filifolia: red flowering gum

Eucalyptus globulus: blue gum
Eucalyptus sideroxylon: red ironbark
Juglans regia: English walnut
Olea europa: olive
Persea americana: avocado
Phoenix canariensis: Canary Island

CALIFORNIA (*continued*)

date palm
Phoenix dactylifera: date palm
Pinus radiata: Monterey pine
Pinus torreyana: Torrey pine
Platanus racemosa: California plane-tree,
　　western sycamore
Prunus amygdalus: almond

Prunus spp.: prune
Pseudotsuga macrocarpa: big-cone
　　Douglas-fir
Quercus agrifolia: California live oak
Quercus douglasii: blue oak
Quercus lobata: California white oak
Quercus suber: cork oak

Quercus wislizenii: interior live oak
Sequoiadendron giganteum: giant
　　sequoia, big tree
Sequoia sempervirens: redwood
Washingtonia filifera: Washington
　　fan palm

TROPICAL FLORIDA

Achras zapota: chewing-gum tree,
　　sapodilla
Bursera simaruba: gumbo limbo
Casuarina equisetifolia: horsetail,
　　beefwood
Ceiba pentandra: silk-cotton tree, kapok
Citrus paradisi: grapefruit
Citrus sinensis: orange
Coccoloba uvifera: sea-grape

Cocos nucifera: coconut
Delonix regia: royal poinciana
Ficus aurea: strangler fig
Ficus benghalensis: banyan
Kigelia pinnata: sausage-tree
Metopium toxiferum: Florida poison
　　wood
Phoenix dactylifera: date palm
Piscidia piscipula: Jamaica dogwood,

fishpoison tree
Rhizophora mangle: red mangrove
**Roystonea regia:* royal palm
Sideroxylon foetidissimum: false-mastic
Swietenia mahogani: West Indies
　　mahogany
Yucca aloifolia: Spanish-bayonet,
　　Spanish dagger

INDEX

(Page numbers in italic refer to illustrations.)